" Live in the sunshine, Swim

Eme

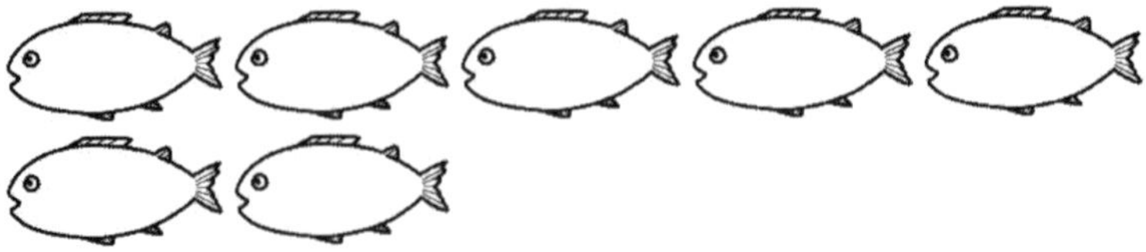

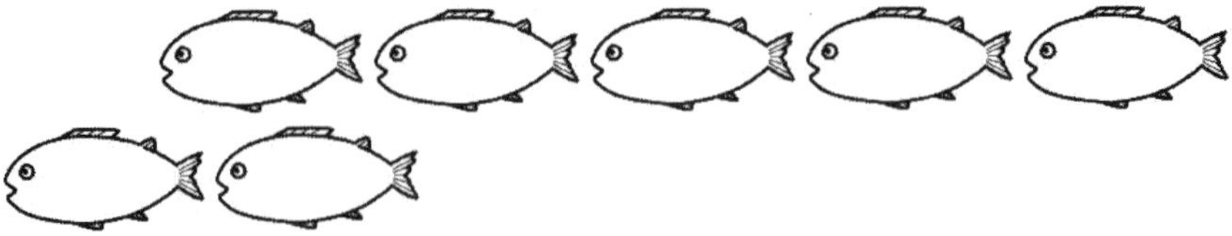

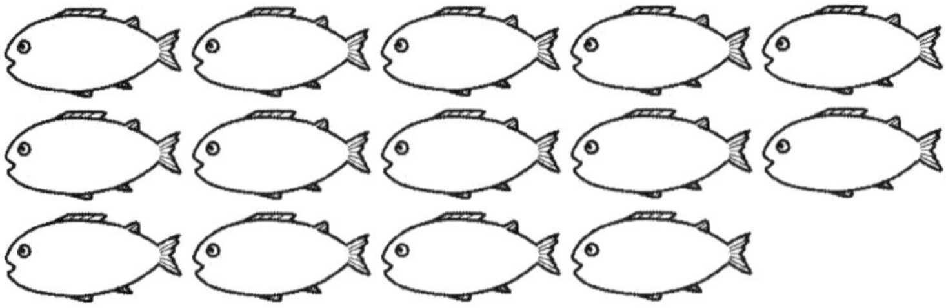

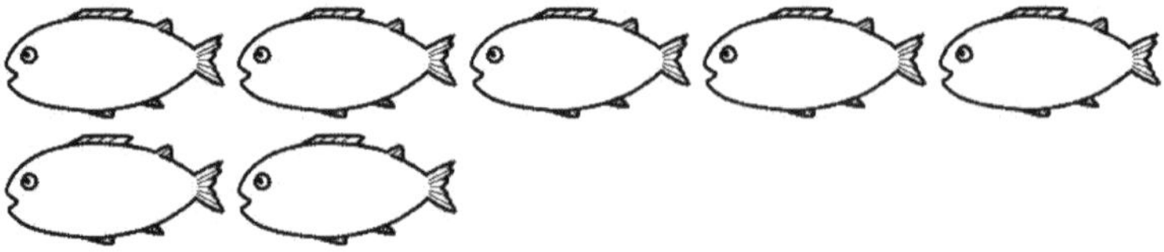

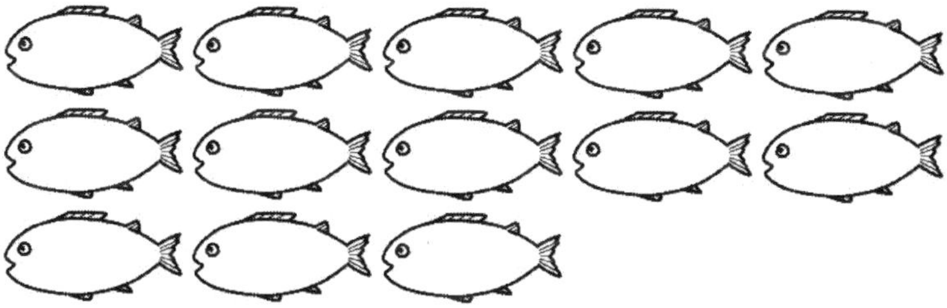

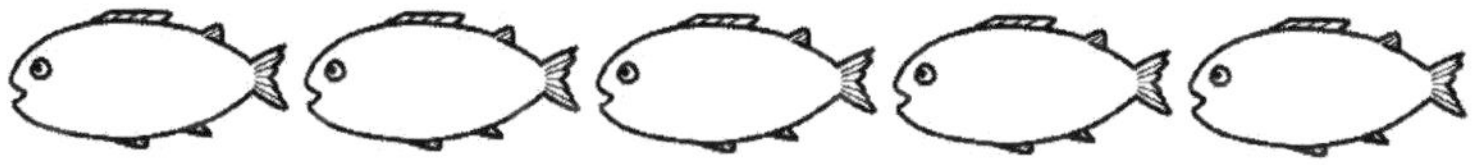

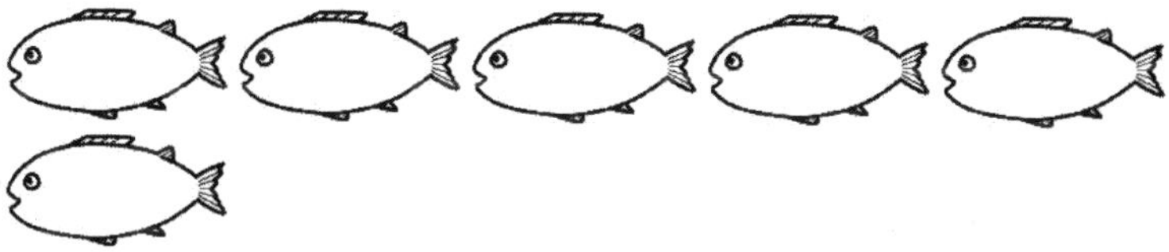

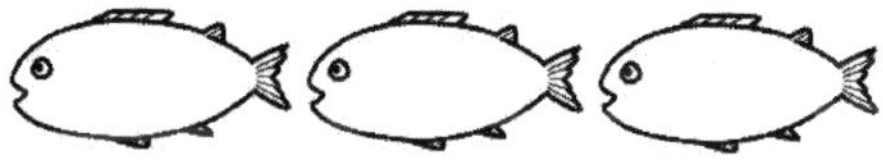

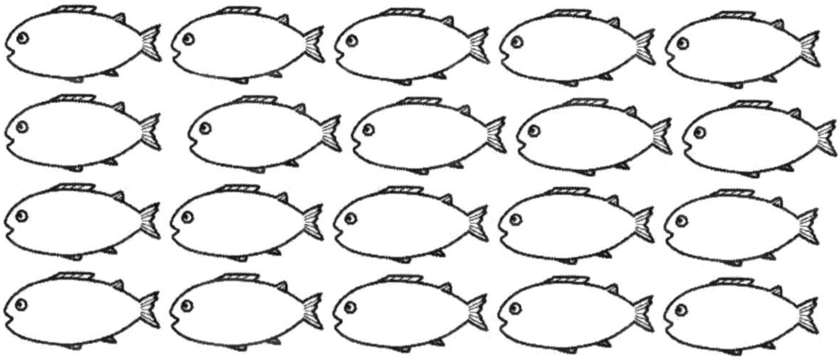

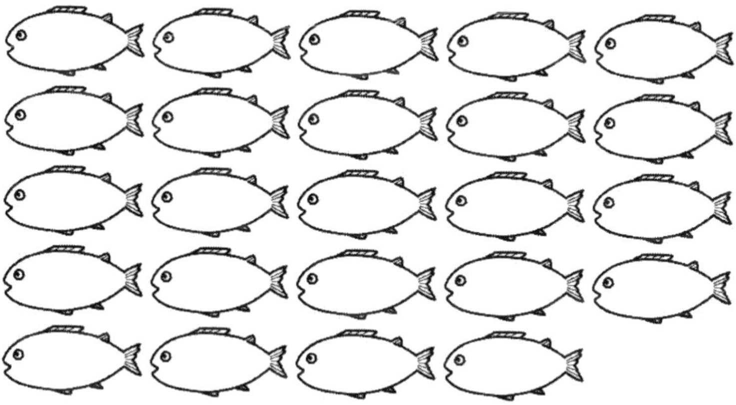

Printed in Great Britain
by Amazon

51950293R00070